THE NATIONAL ANTHEM OF
SOUTH AFRICA

Suzanne,

Take a bit of our history and our
heritage back home with you.

Ludumo Magangane

Magangane

2 July 2016

THE NATIONAL ANTHEM OF SOUTH AFRICA

LUDUMO MAGANGANE

PARTRIDGE

ISBN: Softcover   978-1-4828-2492-6
           eBook   978-1-4828-2491-9

Print information available on the last page.

To order additional copies of this book, contact
Toll Free 0800 990 914 (South Africa)
+44 20 3014 3997 (outside South Africa)
orders.africa@partridgepublishing.com

www.partridgepublishing.com/africa

CONTENTS

Acknowledgements.. vii

Foreword ix

Chapter 1 1

Chapter 2 15

Chapter 3 29

Chapter 4 45

Chapter 5 63

Chapter 6 69

Chapter 7 75

Chapter 8 91

Conclusion 111

Bibliography 113

ACKNOWLEDGEMENTS

1. The South African Music Rights Organisation (SAMRO):

   a. Andre le Roux for facilitating meetings between the Department of National Symbols representative and myself; and for giving permission for me to have access to the SAMRO material on the national anthem.

   b. Noeleen Kotze and Masale Ramonyai for collecting the material for me.

2. Professor Jeanne Zaidel-Rudolph for agreeing to write the Foreword for the book, and for granting me an audience for an interview.

3. Mr Winston Rabotapi for permission from his family, allowing me to write about their great grandfather - Enoch Sontonga.

4. Professor Johan de Villiers for giving me permission to write about his grandfather - Reverend Marthinus Lourence de Villiers.

5. Dr Mothobi Mutloatse for granting me an audience for an interview.

6. Richard Cock for being a source of reference.

7. My dear wife for all the support when I was working through the project.

<u>FOREWORD</u>

South Africa has always possessed a cultural ancestry of great diversity and profound richness. However, due to its turbulent history and social, racial and economic inequalities, our beloved country did not, until relatively recently, reveal its vast store of hidden cultural treasures; its enormous potential for human creative interactivity, cooperation and life-generating empowerment to be found amongst its burgeoning population within the rainbow nation.

It took the vision, courage and remarkable statesmanship of the iconic Nelson Mandela to unite the nation in ways that seemed inconceivable before the spaceship called Democracy landed on our shores. Our beloved Madiba did the unthinkable: he donned the Springbok Rugby shirt and cap, walked on to the field for the World Cup and united a fractured nation in ways that could only have been done by a force beyond Nature. With his prophetic intelligence, Mandela conceptualised the need for a National Anthem that would on the one hand captivate and enthrall and on the other hand placate the vast majority of the population in the 'New South Africa'.

The dictionary definition of a national anthem is a patriotic song or hymn officially adopted as an expression of national identity. Mandela's directive to the newly-constituted Anthem Committee in 1995 focussed on the conscious inclusivity of the brief: the new Anthem needed to embrace as many of the eleven official languages as possible, thus including as many races, cultures and faiths as possible – without offending any group in the process. The final composite version that resulted was the culmination of many fraught journeys and of course many histories. The final version, accepted by Cabinet in 1996 merging *Nkosi Sikelel' iAfrika* and *Die Stem* has not been without controversy – passionate adherents on either side of the divide who either warmly approve of this hybrid form or feel that an entirely new Anthem is desirable. Either way the South African National Anthem has been sung with gusto for nearly twenty years at national and international sporting events, social gatherings and political rallies.

The essence of a national anthem is the setting of words to music. If the words belong to the 'people' and if the cliché that music is a 'universal language' has some veracity, then it is indeed the perfect vehicle to unite the minds and hearts of the inhabitants of South Africa. As an art form, music together with text embodies an intangible beauty and truth not found in the plastic and visual arts – this is the power of music - and the power of a National Anthem in which a prayer is delivered to God to bless Africa and its peoples and protect it from conflict. The Anthem begins in one key but ends in another. This is not only for vocal convenience, but hopefully symbolises the paradigm shift; a modulatory passage and crossing that needed to take place before true democracy could be achieved. Reference is made to the great scenic beauty of the country and it ends with a future vision of a country in which its peoples come together in commitment to peace and freedom. I am honoured to have played an active role in producing the composite version of the Anthem and also to have been invited to contribute this Foreword to a significant book on the South African National Anthem.

Prof Jeanne Zaidel-Rudolph

CHAPTER 1

The National Anthem of South Africa differs from national anthems of other countries firstly because it is in five of the eleven official languages of the republic, while many national anthems are in one language, and secondly because it starts in one key and ends in another, while other national anthems are in one key from the beginning to the end. The first Nguni section and the second Sotho section are both hymnal, have refrains and make a reference to God - asking for blessings and protection. The music of the second section takes off from the original Xhosa composition, but develops differently.

The first line is written in Xhosa, the second and third lines are in Zulu, and the fourth line is again in Xhosa. The Xhosa and Zulu belong to the Nguni African languages.

Nkosi sikelel'iAfrika	Lord bless Africa
Maluphakanyisw'uphondo lwayo	Let it's horn be raised
Yizwa imithandazo yethu	Hear our prayers
Nkosi sikelela thina lusapho lwayo.	Lord bless us we it's offspring.

The next section has a Sotho version of the anthem.

Morena boloka setjhaba sa heso	Lord bless our nation
Ofedise dintwa le matshwenyeho	Banish wars and strife
Oseboloke setjhaba sa heso	Bless our nation
Sechaba sa South Africa.	Of South Africa.

The above sections are in G major.

The third section is in Afrikaans. It is part of the poem "Die Stem van Suid Afrika", and the music is made up of the first four lines of the musical setting of the poem. The lyrics (taking into account the entire verse in the poem) are patriotic.

Uit die blou van onse hemel	Ringing out from our blue heavens
Uit die diepte van ons see	From our deep seas breaking round
Oor ons ewige gebergtes	Over everlasting mountains
Waar die kranse antwoord gee	Where the echoing crags resound.

The closing section is in English. The music of the first two lines is that of lines five and six of the original "Die Stem van Suid Afrika". The music of the last two lines in the English section is that of the last two lines of the first verse of "Die Stem van Suid Afrika". The lyrics evoke a sense of nationalism and patriotism.

Sounds the call to come together
And united we shall stand

Let us strive and fight for freedom

In South Africa our land.

The lyrics in the first stanza are taken from the original Xhosa lyrics as composed by Enoch Mankayi Sontonga. There is no record of who wrote the Sotho adaptation of the hymn, but it was published in 1942 by Moses Mphahlele, who was secretary of the ANC in the Transvaal during the 1920's.

The Afrikaans lyrics are taken from the poem "Die Stem van Suid Afrika" as composed by Cornelius Jacobus Langenhoven, and set to music by Reverend Marthinus Lourens de Villiers.

The English lyrics were composed by Dr Jeanne Zaidel-Rudolph. The national anthem in its form was the culmination of the work done by the Anthem Committee which was chaired by Professor Mzilikazi Khumalo.

The anthem can be sung a capella; can be performed by a symphony orchestra only; a soloist or choir can perform it accompanied by a piano or a symphony orchestra. The orchestral version is the creation of Dr Jeanne Zaidel-Rudolph.

Anyone who wishes to use or adapt the National Anthem in any way whatsoever should make an application to the State Herald in advance at The State Herald, Private Bag X 236, Pretoria 0001.

NATIONAL ANTHEM OF SOUTH AFRICA

C.J. Langenhoven (Afrikaans)
J. Zaidel-Rudolph (English)

E. Sontonga arr. M. Khumalo
M.L. de Villiers arr. Dirkie de Villiers

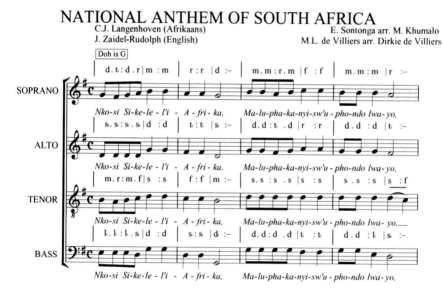

Doh is D
19
m:–. m | f : r | d:–. d | tı : r | d:–. r | r : r | r s:–|–: sı ., sı | d : d | m : m
-so, Se-tjha-ba sa South Af - ri - ca. South Af - ri - ca. Uit die blou van on - se
d:–. d | d : lı | sı:–. sı | sı : sı | sı:–. r | r : r | r s:–|–: sı ., sı | sı : sı | d : d
so, Se-tjha-ba sa South Af - ri - ca. South Af - ri - ca. Uit die blou van on - se
s:–. s | l : f | m:–. m | r : f | m:–. r | r : r | r s:–|–: s ., s | m : m | m : l
so, Se-tjha-ba sa South Af - ri - ca. South Af - ri - ca. Uit die blou van on - se
d:–. dı | fı : fı | sı:–. sı | sı : sı | d:–. r | r : r | r s:–|–: sı ., sı | d : tı | lı : lı
so, Se-tjha-ba sa South Af - ri - ca. South Af - ri - ca. Uit die blou van on - se

4

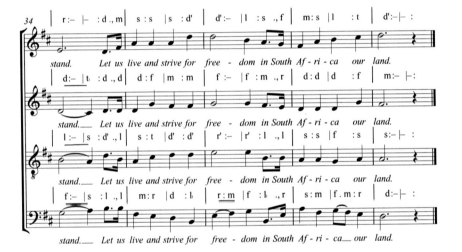

CHAPTER 2

In 1873 Enoch Mankayi Sontonga was born in Uitenhage in the Eastern Cape - born to the Mpinga clan of the Xhosa nation. Not much is known about him except that he trained as a teacher at Lovedale Training Institution. He later became a choir master, composer and photographer.

Enoch left the Cape colony (as it was known then), came to Johannesburg and taught at the Nancefield Methodist Mission School prior to the South African War (Anglo-Boer War). He married Diana Mngqibisa, the daughter of a prominent minister in the African Methodist Episcopal Church, and they had one son - Jefferson Wonga

Sontonga, whose wife Alice came to be known as the "Boxing Granny" because of her love for boxing.

Enoch Sontonga was a preacher in Reverend Mzimba's church. He died on the 18th April 1905 and was buried the following day, the 19th April 1905 in the Black Christian section of the Braamfontein Cemetery.

Nkosi Sikelel'iAfrika is composed

In 1897 Enoch Sontonga composed the hymn "Nkosi Sikelel'iAfrika". The words, in Xhosa, were the following:

Nkosi sikelel'iAfrika	God bless Africa
Maluphakam'uphondo lwayo	Let it's horn be raised
Yiva imithandazo yetu	Hear our prayers
Usisikelele.	and bless us.

Refrain: Yihla Moya, Yihla Moya,	Come down Spirit, Come down Spirit
Yihla Moya oyingcwele.	Come down Holy Spirit.

Nkosi Sikelel'i Africa

Enoch Sontonga

2

The hymn was first sung in 1899 at the ordination of Reverend Boweni, a Shangaan Methodist minister.

Enoch Mankayi Sontonga died on the 18 April 1905 aged 32. On the 18th April 2005 there was a wreath-laying ceremony to mark the 100th anniversary of Sontonga's death.

Popularization of the hymn

On the 8 January 1912, at the first meeting of the South African Native National Congress (SANNC) - the forerunner of the African National Congress (ANC) - in Bloemfontein, "Nkosi Sikelel'iAfrika" was sung immediately after the closing prayer. (Siemon Allen, in his online article The South African National Anthem: A history on record, he states that "Nkosi Sikelel'iAfrika" was sung by the Ohlange Institution choir). Reverend John Langalibalele Dube's Ohlange Zulu Choir, conducted by R.T. Caluza - a choirmaster and composer - popularised the hymn at concerts in Johannesburg and in the

Union of South Africa, and it became a popular church hymn that was also adopted as the anthem at political meetings. (Reverend John Langalibalele Dube was the founder of the Ohlange Institution - a high school in the then Natal, and was the first president of the South African Native National Congress). Professor Cherif Keita of Carleton College in Northfield, Minnesota in the United States of America states in his research about Langalibalele Dube that Nokuthela Dube - Langalibalele's wife - also sang the hymn "Nkosi Sikelel'iAfrika" around the Union of South Africa and abroad during fundraising projects. Both Langalibalele and Nokuthela made sure that Ohlange Institute students got to know and sang "Nkosi Sikelel'iAfrika". The Dube's finally published the hymn as "Prayer for the Children of Ohlange" in 1911 in their book Amagama Abantu. They believed that the hymn was a Gospel of their deep belief that Africa has its own destiny from God and only Africa could control that destiny by sounding its own horn, as Sontonga said. The Dube's used the hymn for basic spiritual and political objectives.

Solomon Plaatje, one of South Africa's greatest writers and a founding member of the ANC, was the first to have the hymn recorded in London on 16 October 1923, accompanied by Sylvia Colenso on piano.

From 1925 "Nkosi Sikelel'iAfrika" became the official anthem for the African National Congress - it became their closing anthem for their meetings.

Samuel Edward Krune Mqhayi - a Xhosa poet - added seven verses (in 1927) to the one verse that Enoch Sontonga had composed.

Sikelela iNkosi zetu;	Bless our chiefs
Zimkumbule umDali wazo;	May they remember their Creator;
Zimoyike zezimhlonele,	Fear Him and revere Him,
Azisikelele.	That He may bless them.

Sikelel'amadod'esizwe,	Bless the public men,
Sikelela kwa nomlisela	Bless also the youth
Ulitwal'ilizwe	That they may carry
ngomonde,	the land with patience,
Uwusikelele.	and that Thou mayst
	bless them.

Sikelel'amakosikazi;	Bless the wives;
Nawo	And also all young
onk'amanenekazi;	women;
Pakamisa	Lift up all the young
wonk'umtinjana	girls
Uwusikelele.	And bless them.

Sikelela abafundisi	Bless the ministers
Bemvaba zonke zelizwe;	of all churches of this land;
Ubatwese ngoMoya Wako	Endue them with Thy Spirit
Ubasikelele.	And bless them.

Sikelel'ulimo nemfuyo;	Bless agriculture and stock raising;
Gxota zonk'indlala nezifo;	Banish all famine and diseases;
Zalisa ilizwe ngempilo	Fill the land with good health
Ulisikelele.	And bless it.

Sikelel'amalinge etu	Bless our efforts
Awomanyano	of union and self-uplift,
nokuzaka,	
Awemfundo	of education and
nemvisiswano	mutual understanding
Uwasikelele.	And bless them.

Nkosi sikelel'iAfrika;	Lord, bless Africa;
Cima bonk'ubugwenxa	Blot out all its
bayo	wickedness
Nezigqito, nezono zayo	And its transgressions
	and sins,
Uyisikelele.	And bless it.

The hymn - all verses - was first published in 1927 by Lovedale Press in pamphlet form. It was also published in a newspaper, Umteteli wabantu on 11 June 1927 and in a Xhosa poetry book for schools entitled ImiHobe nemiBongo (Sheldon Press). It was included in Incwadi Yamaculo ase Rabe (Presbyterian Xhosa Hymn Book), issued by Lovedale Press in 1929.

The ANC continued using "Nkosi Sikelel'iAfrika", and the hymn became a Pan-African liberation anthem and was later adopted as the national anthem of Zambia, Tanzania (Mungu ibariki Afrika – Swahili), Namibia and Zimbabwe (Ishe komborera Africa – Shona) after these countries became independent. Zimbabwe and Namibia have since adopted new national anthems. In other African countries throughout Southern Africa, the hymn was sung as part of the anti-colonial movement. It includes versions in Chichewa (Malawi and Zambia).

On the 26th October 1976, "Nkosi Sikelel'iAfrika was proclaimed the National Anthem of Transkei on their becoming independent, in Supplement 4 to the Republic of Transkei Constitution. (Dr Yvonne Huskisson, SABC - recorded 29/11/76).

In Finland the same melody is used as the children's psalm Kuule Isä Taivaan (Hear, Heavenly Father). The first part of the hymn has appeared in the hymn book of the Evangelical Lutheran Church of Finland since 1985 with lyrics by Jaakko Löytty. In Kenya, Mang'u High School uses a translation, Mungu Ibariki Mang'u High, as its school anthem.

Sue A. Cock made a setting for voice and piano from the choral arrangement by Professor Mzilikazi Khumalo, which was published in the African Arts Trust in 1994.

CHAPTER 3

On the 13 August 1873 Cornelis Jacobus Langenhoven, better known as Sagmoedige Neelsie (Gentle Neelsie) or Kerneels, was born at Hoeko, Ladismith in the Cape Colony and later moved to Oudtshoorn where he became its most famous resident. (Reader note that Enoch Sontonga and C.J. Langenhoven were born in the same year in the Cape Colony!)

The poem "Die Stem van Suid Afrika" is composed

In May 1918 C.J. Langenhoven composed the poem "Die Stem van Suid Afrika". This formed part of his

literary endeavours at the time to develop the young
language - Afrikaans.

First verse

Die Stem van Suid Afrika	The Voice of South Africa
Uit die blou van onse hemel,	Ringing out from our blue heavens,
Uit die diepte van ons see,	From our deep seas breaking round,
Oor ons ewige gebergtes Waar die kranse antwoord gee.	Over everlasting mountains Where the echoing crags resound.
Deur ons ver verlate vlaktes	From our plains where creaking wagons,
Met die kreun van ossewa.	Cut their trails into the earth.

Ruis die stem van ons geliefde,	Calls the spirit of our country,
Van ons land Suid Afrika.	Of the land that gave us birth.
Ons sal antwoord op jou roepstem,	At thy call we shall not falter,
Ons sal offer wat jy vra:	Firm and steadfast we shall stand,
Ons sal lewe, ons sal sterwe,	At thy will to live or perish,
Ons vir jou, Suid Afrika.	O South Africa, dear land.

Second verse

In die merg van ons gebeente,	In our body and our spirit,
in ons hart en siel en gees,	In our inmost heart held fast;

In ons roem op ons verlede, In the promise of our

          future,

In ons hoop op wat sal And the glory of our past;

wees.

In ons wil en werk en In our will, our work, our

wandel,   striving,

Van ons wieg tot aan ons From the cradle to the

graf.   grave-

Deel geen ander land ons There's no land that shares

liefde,   our loving,

Vaderland, ons sal die adel, Thou has borne us and we

          know thee,

Van jou naam met   May our deeds to all

eere dra: proclaim

Waar en trou as Afrikaners, Our enduring love and

          service

Kinders van Suid-Afrika.

To thy honour and thy name.

Third verse

In die songloed van ons somer,
In the golden warmth of summer,

in ons winternag se kou,
In the chill of winter's air,

In die lente van ons liefde,
In the surging life of springtime,

in die lanfer van ons rou;
In the autumn of despair;

By die klink van huw'liksklokkies,
When the wedding bells are chiming,

by die kluit-klap op die kis.
Or when those we love do depart,

Streel jou stem ons nooit verniet nie,
Thou dost know us for thy children

Weet jy waar jou kinders is	And dost take us to thy heart
Op jou roep se ons nooit nee nie,	Loudly peals the answering chorus;
Se ons altyd, altyd ja:	We are thine, and we shall stand,
Om te lewe, om te sterwe -	Be it life or death, to answer
Ja, ons kom, Suid-Afrika,	To thy call, beloved land.

Fourth verse

Op U Almag vas vertrouend	In thy power, Almighty, trusting,
het ons vadere gebou;	Did our father build of old;
Skenk ook ons die krag, O Here!	Strengthen then, O Lord, their children
Om te handhaaf en te hou,	To defend, to love, to hold-
Dat die erwe van ons vadere	That the heritage they gave us

Vir ons kinders erwe bly;	For our children yet may be;
Knegte van die	Bondsmen only to the
Allerhoogste,	Highest
Teen die hele wereld vry.	And before the whole world free.
Soos ons vadere	As our fathers trusted
vertrou het,	humbly,
Leer ook ons vertrou, O	Teach us, Lord to trust Thee
Heer:	still;
Met ons land en met ons	Guard our land and guide
nasie	our people
Sal dit wel wees, God	In Thy way to do Thy will.
regeer.	

Initially Langenhoven had written three verses. He added the fourth verse at the request of the government to bolster the religious theme.

"Die Stem van Suid Afrika" becomes the official national anthem

In 1919 a Cape newspaper "Die Burger", which incidentally was founded by Langenhoven, sponsored a competition for music to be composed to the poem, but initial attempts were unsatisfactory to Langenhoven.

"Die Stem van Suid Afrika" was ultimately set to music by the Reverend Marthinus Lourens de Villiers in 1921, who at the time was a minister in the Dutch Reformed Church and was also a music teacher at Wepener in the Free State.

Die Stem Van Suid-Afrika

C.J. Langenhoven · Doh is F · M.L. De Villiers arr. Dirkie De Villiers

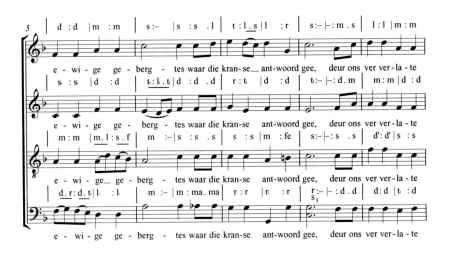

2

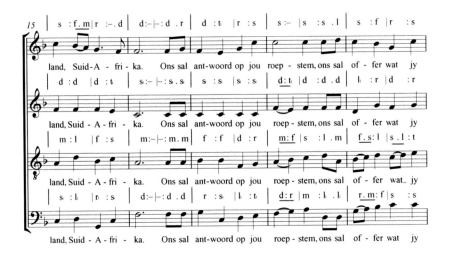

land, Suid-A-fri - ka.   Ons sal ant-woord op jou roep - stem, ons sal of - fer wat   jy

land, Suid - A - fri - ka.   Ons sal ant-woord op jou   roep - stem, ons sal of - fer wat   jy

land, Suid, A - fri - ka.   Ons sal ant-woord op jou   roep - stem, ons sal of - fer wat_ jy

land, Suid - A - fri - ka.   Ons sal ant-woord op jou   roep - stem, ons sal of - fer wat   jy

It's first public performance was on the 31 May 1928 - on Union Day - at the official hoisting of the national flag in Cape Town. In 1936 "Die Federasie van Afrikaanse Kulturvereenigings" unanimously selected the poem by Langenhoven and the music of de Villiers as the winners of a competition to find the best lyrics and music for an official National Anthem. In 1952 an English translation was selected from more than 220 submissions, and it was accepted for official use. "Die Stem van Suid Afrika" was the co-national anthem with "God Save The Queen/King between 1936 and 1957.

On the 2nd May 1957 the then government announced that "Die Stem van Suid Afrika" was the official national anthem. From 1957 till 1995 "Die Stem van Suid Afrika" became the national anthem of white South Africa, and only the first verse was sung.

Langenhoven was instrumental in pushing for the acceptance of Afrikaans as a language in general, and as the first language in schools instead of Dutch. This culminated in the Afrikaans language being used officially in parliament in 1925, (the same year the African National Congress adopted "Nkosi Sikelel'iAfrika" to be sung at the end of their meetings), and by 1927 was recognised as an official language of South Africa, together with English.

CHAPTER 4

"Nkosi Sikelel'iAfrika undergoes changes

A Zulu version of "Nkosi Sikelel'iAfrika" later came about:

Nkosi sikelel'iAfrika	Lord bless Africa
Maluphakanyisw'uphondo lwayo	Let her horn be raised
Yizwa imithandazo yethu	Hear our prayers
Nkosi sikelela thina lusapho lwayo.	Lord bless us her children.

The fourth line also changed from "Usisikelele" to "Nkosi sikelela thina lusapho lwayo". "Sikelela" is a Xhosa word, but was retained instead of translating it to "busisa" - which is Zulu.

The refrain which was "Yihla moya oyingcwele" (Come down Holy Spirit) changed to "Woza moya oyingcwele". "Yihla" in Xhosa means "Come down", whereas "Woza" in Zulu just means "Come". A direct translation of "Yihla" to Zulu would be "Yehla", but "Woza" sounds better musically than "Yehla" (if that was the consideration).

In Enoch Sontonga's original version, the call by sopranos (Yihla Moya) takes a full bar, and the response by the altos, tenors and basses starts in the next bar. The response in the version with Zulu translations starts in the third beat of the same bar where the call starts. Another version has altos and tenors singing "Sikelela, Nkosi Sikelela" when basses sing "Woza Moya, Woza". The new refrain has more music than Enoch Sontonga's refrain. Sontonga's refrain ends with "Yihla Moya oyingcwele" (Come down Holy Spirit), whereas the new refrain continues to "Nkosi Sikelela thina lusapho lwayo" (Lord bless us her children), which is a repeat of the last line of the first stanza.

Some renditions of the hymn in the then Natal went further and changed "Maluphakanyisw'uphondo lwayo" (Let her horn be raised) to "Maluphakanyisw'udumo lwayo" (Let her fame be raised). The key to this Zulu version also changed from B flat major to G major.

A Sotho version was added to the hymn - with the following lyrics:

Morena boloka setjhaba   God preserve our
sa heso   nation

| O fedise dintwa le matshwenyeho | Let there be no strife and hardships |
| O se boloke Morena setjhaba sa heso. | Preserve it Lord - our nation. |

As indicated in chapter 1, there is no record of who composed the Sotho version, but it was published by Moses Mphahlele in 1942 in the Morija Mission, Basutoland (as it was known then).

The last addition to the hymn were the words:

| Makube njalo kuze kube ngunaphakade | Let it be so forever. |

This addition was like a coda, and it would be repeated during renditions.

The new format of the hymn was therefore the following:

Nkosi sikelel'iAfrika	God bless Africa
Maluphakanyisw'uphondo	Let it's horn be
lwayo	raised
Yizwa imithandazo yethu	Hear our prayers
Nkosi sikelela thina	Lord bless us we it's
lusapho lwayo.	offspring.

Refrain: Woza moya	Come spirit
Woza moya oyingcwele	Come Holy Spirit
Nkosi sikelela thina	Lord bless us her
lusapho lwayo	children.

Morena boloka setjhaba sa heso	God preserve our nation
O fedise dintwa lè matshwenyeho	Let there be no strife and hardships
O se boloke Morena	Preserve it Lord
Setjhaba sa heso	our nation
Makube njalo kuze kube phakade	Let it be so forever

Nkosi Sikelel'iAfrika

Enoch Mankayi Sontonga

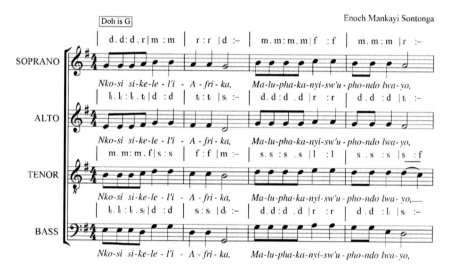

For decades during the apartheid period in South Africa the above version of the hymn was considered by many to be the unofficial national anthem of South Africa, representing the suffering of the oppressed. It would be sung as a closing prayer for political meetings, civic functions and choir competitions. The hymn has also been recorded by: the ANC's Amandla Choir in exile, Paul Simon and Mirriam Makeba, Ladysmith Black Mambazo, Boom Shaka (in kwaito style), Osibisa, Oliver Mtukudzi (the Shona version that was once the anthem of Zimbabwe) and the Mahotella Queens.

CHAPTER 5

Nkosi! The Healing Song

In 1992 Mothobi Mutloatse wrote NKOSI! The Healing Song, to celebrate the 95th anniversary of "Nkosi Sikelel'iAfrika". The programme was a mixed bag which climaxed with a choral rendition of "Nkosi Sikelel'iAfrika" by Imilonji ka Ntu - one of the leading choirs in South Africa. The performance highlighted the fact that the hymn was not only sung in South Africa, but was also sung in Zambia, Zimbabwe and Tanzania (The Namibian version was not included in this performance). It was performed at the Witwatersrand University's Great

Hall by an array of artists, in the same year South Africa was involved in the Convention for a Democratic South Africa (CODESA).

Already on people's lips was the question - which anthem was the new South Africa going to adopt? There were those who thought that "Nkosi Sikelel'iAfrika" would be an obvious choice.

Mothobi Mutloatse asked some of the leaders in the Black community to make entries in the programme of the production NKOSI! The Healing Song. The following are extracts from those entries:

"Nkosi! The Healing Song couldn't have come at a more appropriate time. We hope it will bring about the peace and reconciliation that we're all yearning for, among all the people particularly Black South Africans." - by Gobingca G. Mxadana - music director of Imilonji ka Ntu.

"I believe it is inevitable that Nkosi Sikelel'iAfrika will become the official anthem of South Africa, a prayer for our land, and for all the people of Africa." - by the late Dr Aggrey Klaaste, who was the editor of the Sowetan newspaper at the time.

"Sikelel'iAfrika is a recognition that African people are one people, one nation, the fragmentation, of the continent is artificial." - by the late Dr Nthato Motlana.

"We say that Nkosi Sikelel'iAfrika should be adopted as the national anthem of liberated South Africa, and hope that reason will prevail over sentiment when the issue comes up for discussion." - by Professor JS Mohlamme of the Department of History at Vista University.

"To most of us, South African Blacks, and especially to those who live in the townships, this song is a true African song, and fit for our national anthem." - by Professor

Mzilikazi Khumalo, one of the foremost composers of Zulu choral music and then Professor of African Languages at the Witwatersrand University.

In 1997 during the centenary celebration of Nkosi Sikelel'iAfrika, there were a number of performances of Nkosi! The Healing Song at the Witwatersrand University's Great Hall. The Post Office issued a special stamp in Sontonga's honour on Heritage Day.

[During an interview I had with Dr Mothobi Mutloatse, he indicated that actually Moses Mphahlele composed "Morena Boloka Setjhaba Sa Heso". This piece of crucial information he said he got from Moses Mphahlele's family members.]

The three following paragraphs are quoted from an article which had nothing to do with the above-mentioned performance, but I am quoting them because they resonate with the sentiments expressed above. They are from an article from the Sunday Times of October 31 1993 by Professor Tim Couzens, an historian and winner of the Alan Paton Award for his book "Tramp Royal". The title of the article was 'Anthem has a solid claim to being national':

"It is a curious fact that, amid all the controversy over the proposed national anthem, few people know that it was Enoch Sontonga who wrote the hymn; even fewer know anything about the man himself. Yet such knowledge may help us out of our difficulties and make the hymn more acceptable to a wider range of people as an anthem."

In recent years the hymn has been adopted as the national anthem by other countries: it is surely a matter of pride that we should now reclaim our own."

"And that is also why Nkosi Sikelel'iAfrika must be retained as the truly national anthem. We owe it to Mr Sontonga. We owe it to ourselves."

CHAPTER 6

Enoch Sontonga's grave is discovered

There were endeavours by various interested parties to find Enoch Sontonga's grave. One such endeavour was by Dr Mothobi Mutloatse - a South African author. He says 'I tried to trace the gravesite of Tat'uSontonga in Braamfontein, poring over the register at the Braamfontein Cemetery over several afternoons, without success. All I found were references to the burial of "Kaffir this", and "Kaffir that...." MaSontonga consoled me by saying that, as long as we knew that Tata was buried there, then "that's all that mattered Son." Even then, she admonished me - "what's the difference between one grave and another?" "Yes, makhulu," I had replied in disappointment.'

In 1994 the National Monuments Council became aware that Sontonga was possibly buried in the Braamfontein Cemetery, Johannesburg. Over the years, several unsuccessful attempts had been made to locate Sontonga's grave in the Braamfontein cemetery. However, it was not until Hal Shaper (a songwriter and music producer from Cape Town) who had been researching the history of "Nkosi Sikelel'iAfrika" prompted the cemetery officials to look for an entry in the burial register under Enoch, rather than Sontonga, and to look at burial records for 1905, that success was achieved. The register at Braamfontein lists the date of burial as 19 April 1905 in Plot No 4885. Confirmation that this was indeed Enoch Sontonga's grave was subsequently found in a notice in the newspaper,

Iimvo Zabansundu, which stated that Enoch Sontonga had died unexpectedly on 18 April 1905 in Johannesburg. The newspaper report also noted that he was born in Uitenhage in the Eastern Cape and that he had one son.

To establish exactly where Plot No 4885 was, became a major undertaking. "At the time, it was common for the surnames of blacks not to be shown on cemetery records. Senior administrative assistant at the cemetery Mercia Erasmus discovered that a 32-year-old "Enoch Kaffir" had been buried in the Christian part of the cemetery in 1905." [From a newspaper report entitled 'Writer finds Nkosi composer's grave' by Tendai Dumbutshena - name of paper and date not discipherable because it is a photocopy.] The search was complicated by the fact that during the early 1960s that particular section of the cemetery, comprising 10 acres, was levelled and landscaped. Mr Allan Buff, Regional Manager (Parks and Cemeteries) of the Greater Johannesburg Transitional Metropolitan Council (GJTMC), did a detailed research on the existing records that took over a year to complete. He studied the site plan for a proposed park in 1960, the burial concept plan of 1898, an area site plan of 1909, an infra-red burial plan of 1969 and the aerial photograph of 1938 and merged all the information gathered to identify the area in which the grave was located. Identification of the grave itself was part of a second stage in which Professor Tom Huffman of the Department of Archaeology at the University of the Witwatersrand was contracted to do a shallow archaeological excavation to confirm the burial spacing. Finally, from the interpolation of all the data, a site plan was drawn identifying the plot considered to be the grave of Enoch Sontonga.

After Enoch Sontonga's grave was located, it was declared a National Monument on 24 September 1996, Heritage

Day. It was unveiled by then President Nelson Rolihlahla Mandela. At the ceremony, the Order of Meritorious Service (Gold) was bestowed on Sontonga posthumously, received by his granddaughter, Mrs Ida Rabotapi.

The road previously known as Show Ground Road was renamed "Enoch Sontonga Avenue" and a portion of the cemetery was named Enoch Sontonga Memorial Park.

The Sowetan Massed Choir Festival of 1997 also recognised the contribution by Enoch Sontonga. Mrs Rabotapi again accepted the award on behalf of her grandfather during the festival held at the Standard Bank Arena.

CHAPTER 7

Nkosi Sikelel'iAfrika at the Massed Choir Festival

From the mid-eighties South Africa began experiencing political upheavals and mass murders. This caused the then state president P.W. Botha to declare a state of emergency in 1986. This however did not help matters - the violence escalated and continued unabated.

It was at this time that the late Dr Aggrey Klaaste, who was the editor of the newspaper Sowetan at the time, proposed a nation building concept. The idea behind the concept was to identify people in various African, Coloured and

Indian communities around South Africa who were making positive contributions towards nation building. The people were nominated by their communities and would come to Johannesburg to be honoured.

Another important aspect of this nation building concept was the Massed Choir Festival. A choir of thousand voices would be put together and would be accompanied by a nation building orchestra in presenting a mixed programme of Western and African composed songs plus arrangements of African folk songs. The Massed Choir Festival took place at the Standard Bank Arena in Johannesburg from 1989. It was called the Sowetan Massed Choir Festival. Some people thought that Dr Klaaste was crazy to introduce a choral festival when South Africa was burning.

Whilst working at the Witwatersrand University, Professor Khumalo had the fortune to receive from a colleague of his - Professor Tim Couzens of the Department of African Studies at the same university - a set of original "Lovedale" songs, among which was a full copy of Enoch Sontonga's "Nkosi Sikelel'iAfrika". This 'gift' enabled Professor Khumalo to introduce "Nkosi Sikelel'iAfrika" (the version that is in chapter four) to the Sowetan Massed Choir Festival where he was a music director together with Richard Cock, in 1990.

Professor Khumalo had to effect a few changes to the commonly used version of "Nkosi Sikelel'iAfrika" in order to align it with Sontonga's original version. The changes were mostly in the "Nkosi Sikelel'iAfrika" section. Firstly he changed the key of the song from G major to key B flat major, thus aligning it with Sontonga's original key. In bars 3 and 4 he retained

Sontonga's musical setting and the original lyrics "maluphakam'uphondo lwayo" instead of any of what was the commonly used forms: "Maluphakanyisw'uphondo lwayo"; "Maluphakamisw'uphondo lwayo"; "Maluphakanyisw'udumo lwayo" etc. The image in Sontonga's lyrics of Africa rising with it's horns was more powerful according to Professor Khumalo, than that of a seemingly dislocated horn being raised or even of Africa's name being exalted. In bars 7 - 10, he also retained Sontonga's words "Usisikelele (twice)" instead of "Nkosi sikelela (twice)." In bar 5, however, he chose the commonly used "Yizwa" (Zulu) instead of Sontonga's "Yiva" (Xhosa), and in bars 15 and 16 he also used "Woza Moya", which was more commonly used than Sontonga's "Yihla Moya." In the same bars he retained Sontonga's original musical format. In bars 11 - 14 and 20 - 23 Professor Khumalo used the commonly used words and melody "Nkosi

Sikelela, thina lusapho lwayo", both of which were not found in Sontonga's original version.

The melody and harmony in this version were kept almost identical to what Sontonga had put down, the only difference being in the melody of the basses in bars 1 and 5, where the bass notes anticipated those of bars 24, 26, 28 and 30 of the "Morena Boloka" section, thus helping to bind the two sections more securely.

From 1990 to 1996 the Massed Choir sang this format, without accompaniment.

THE AFRICAN NATIONAL ANTHEM

Enoch Sontonga

2

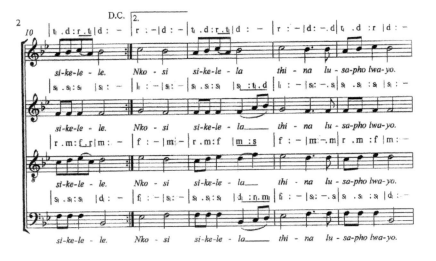

si-ke-le - le.   Nko - si   si-ke-le - la   thi - na   lu - sa-pho lwa-yo.

D.S.

20

%

| r :– | d :– | t,.d : r | d :– | | r :– | d :– .d | t,.d : r | d :– | | d.d : d .r | m :.m .m |

Nko - si   si-ke-le - la   thi - na   lu - sa-pho lwa-yo.   Mo-re-na bo-lo-ka se-

| l, :– | s, :– | s, .s, : s, | s, :– t.d | | l, :– | s, :– .s, | s, .s, : s, | s, :– | | l, .l, : l, .t, | d : d .d |

Nko - si   si-ke-le - la_____   thi - na   lu - sa-pho lwa-yo.   Mo-re-na bo-lo-ka se-

| f :– | m :– | r .m : f | m : s | | f :– | m :– .m | r .m : f | m :– | | m.m : m .f | s : s .s |

Nko - si   si-ke-le - la_____   thi - na   lu - sa-pho lwa-yo.   Mo-re-na bo-lo-ka se-

| f, :– | s, :– | s, .s, : s, | d, : η, .m, | | f, :– | s, :– .s, | s, .s, : s, | d, :– | | l, .l, : l, .s, | d : d .d |

Nko - si   si-ke-le - la_____   thi - na   lu - sa-pho lwa-yo.   Mo-re-na bo-lo - ka se-

4

6

49

CHAPTER 8

Events leading to the new national anthem

On the 2nd February 1990 then President F.W. de Klerk unbanned all political organisations, and on the 9th February 1990 he released Nelson Mandela - unconditionally - from Victor Vester prison. These two events had a profound effect on the political landscape of South Africa. They also helped to soften the attitude of the world to apartheid South Africa. One of the results of these events was the readmission of South Africa to international sporting competitions.

The readmission to international sporting competitions also came with awkward moments. At an international rugby game between the Springboks and the All Blacks in New Zealand in 1992, "Die Stem van Suid Afrika" was sung. This angered the ANC, and the organisation issued a statement that "Die Stem" should not be sung when our national teams play international games. At the Barcelona Olympics in the same year Schiller's "Ode to Joy" set to the music of Beethoven was played for the South African sporting men and women, in the place of a South African national anthem.

Another major political milestone occurred in South Africa - the Convention for a Democratic South Africa began at the World Trade Centre in Kempton Park in 1991. The process continued in 1992 and was followed by the Multi-Party Negotiation Process in April 1993. It produced South Africa's Interim Constitution, and

Professor Elize Botha was appointed chairman of the Commission on National Symbols by the Multiparty Negotiating Council.

The council invited submissions from the public for the adoption of a new National Anthem. A Sub-Committee was appointed to oversee the process, and Professor Musa Xulu was part of that Sub-Committee. Later Professor Mzilikazi Khumalo was also invited to be part of the Sub-Committee. Although more than 200 proposed anthems were received, and none was considered suitable.

The Sub-Committee then suggested the combining of "Die Stem van Suid Afrika" and "Nkosi Sikelel'iAfrika" to constitute the new National Anthem. This proposal was accepted by the Negotiating Council, and this combination of the two works was, at first, the official National Anthem from 1994. A proclamation issued by the (then) State President on 20 April 1994 in terms of the provisions of Section 248 (1) together with Section 2 of the Constitution of the Republic of South Africa, 1993 (Act 200 of 1993), stated that the Republic of South Africa would have two national anthems. They were Nkosi Sikelel'iAfrika and The Call of South Africa (Die Stem van Suid-Afrika).

The long combined anthem is shortened

However, it was immediately apparent that the Anthem was extremely long. In compliance with the decision taken by the cabinet on the 9th November 1994, Dr Ben Ngubane, then Minister of Arts, Culture, Science and Technology, called into being a Committee to produce a shortened version in both choral and instrumental settings. The members of the committee were:

Ms Anna Bender

Prof. Elize Botha

Mr Richard Cock

Prof. Mzilikazi Khumalo (Chairman)

Prof. Mazisi Kunene

Prof. John Lenake

Prof. Fatima Meer

Prof. Khabi Mngoma

Dr. Wally Serote

Prof. Johan de Villiers

Dr. Jeanne Zaidel-Rudolph

Mr Dolph Havemann of the Directorate of Arts and Culture was appointed Secretary of the Committee.

The Anthem Committee commenced work on the 10th February 1995. In welcoming the committee, Dr Ngubane said "We must take the precious heritage of our people and use this as a cornerstone to build our common future and destiny".

The first problem the Committee attended to was that of the length of the combined anthems. A study of twenty-seven national anthems gave an average duration of 1 minute 47 seconds each. The longest anthem in this group - that of Switzerland - lasted 2 minutes 40 seconds. The South African Anthem on the other hand was 5 minutes and 4 seconds! The shortening process was that of removing repetitions and also leaving out those sections that had words considered unacceptable by some sections of our community.

The section "Makube njalo" was the first target for excision, since it was not really part of 'Nkosi Sikelel'iAfrika' or 'Morena Boloka'. In fact, "Makube njalo" was an affirmation used at the conclusion of hymns in some African churches.

The Council of Muslim Theologians made a submission against the retention of the "Woza Moya" section. This refrain is a reference to the Christian concept of the Holy Trinity, and, by singing it, they submitted, Muslims would be violating their fundamental creed (Kalema), and thereby defying the very essence of Monotheism, that is the Oneness of Allah. Thus, the "Woza Moya" section was left out.

Repetitions in 'Nkosi Sikelel'iAfrika' and 'Morena boloka' were also left out, and this gave the committee the following shortened version of the entire "Nkosi Sikelel'iAfrika" component:

Nkosi Sikelel'iAfrika	Lord bless Africa
Maluphakanyisw'uphondo lwayo	Let it's horn be raised
Yizwa imithandazo yethu	Hear our prayers
Nkosi Sikelela thina lusapho lwayo	Lord bless us her offspring
Morena boloka setjhaba sa heso	Lord bless our nation
Ofedise dintwa le matshwenyeho	Let there be no strife and hardships
O se boloke, O se boloke	Preserve it, preserve it
Setjhaba sa heso	Our nation
Setjhaba sa South Africa	The South African nation

In the last line of the Southern Sotho section the committee introduced the words 'sa South Africa' in place of 'sa heso' or 'sa Africa' which had been commonly used forms. The committee felt a need for diluting the Pan-African flavour in "Nkosi Sikelel'iAfrika" (God bless Africa) by referring to the South African nation rather than simply as 'our nation' (setjhaba sa heso) or loosely as 'the African nation' (setjhaba sa Afrika).

The words and music of "Die Stem van Suid Afrika" consisted of twelve lines:

Uit die blou van onse hemel

Uit die diepte van ons see

Oor ons ewige gebergtes

Waar die kranse antwoord gee,

Oor ons ver-verlate vlaktes

Met die kreun van ossewa

Ruis die stem van ons geliefde,

Van ons land Suid Afrika.

Ons sal antwoord op jou roepstem,

Ons sal offer wat jy vra

Ons sal lewe, ons sal sterwe

Ons vir jou Suid Afrika.

Some sections had also to be left out of 'Die Stem' in order to maintain balance. The obvious target was the four-line segment incorporating reference to the Great Trek (met die kreun van ossewa), since this was the experience of only one section of the community. Lines 5 to 8 were thus left out. Then the committee felt that the last four lines in this component should be in English, so that those members of our community who had a closer association with English rather than with Afrikaans or African languages, should feel included rather than excluded in the national anthem of their country. Dr Jeanne Zaidel-Rudolph proposed the English words. The last four lines were therefore changed to:

We can hear the land rejoicing,

With a voice not heard before

Let the people of our country

Live in peace for evermore.

The next point to be considered was the order in which these components would be sung. No official decision had been taken on this matter, and, in the few renditions that the committee had heard, the singers had started with 'Die Stem'. The committee, however, felt that it would be better to reverse the order, since it was the music of 'Die Stem' that produced a climatic ending.

The committee then looked at the keys of the two compositions. 'Nkosi Sikelel'iAfrika' was composed in B flat major and 'Die Stem' was composed in E flat major, but these keys were found too high for communal singing. The songs had been commonly sung in G major and D major respectively, and these are the keys the committee finally decided on. But there was a need for a simple musical 'bridge' to facilitate an easy change of key. This was provided by adding in a bar of music in which each syllable of 'South Africa' is sung in unison to the note A, which is the supertonic (reh in Tonic Sol-fa) of key G major, while also functioning as the dominant (soh in Tonic Sol-fa) of the new key - D major.

This concluded the committee's work on the shortened choral version of the national anthem. For the orchestration, which would be used either either as an accompaniment to the singing or as an instrumental rendition on its own, the committee is indebted to Professor (then Doctor) Jeanne Zaidel-Rudolph. She produced a version for full symphony orchestra, and also produced a version for voice and piano.

Submissions by the anthem committee

The first submission of the shortened choral version to the Cabinet was made on the 4th April 1995 by the chairman and secretary of the committee. The cabinet expressed satisfaction with the music of the anthem, but they asked for further work on the English words. They felt that the suggested words painted a fine picture of the festive, optimistic mood prevailing in the country, but they did very little in urging our people to commit themselves to the building of a nation upholding the tenets of our hard-won freedom. They asked the committee to meet again and consider changes to the English words and other possible options of setting the Afrikaans and English words.

The shortened anthem was premiered at the Cape Town Caltex Massed Choir Festival on the 7th May 1995.

The committee held their second meeting on 9th May 1995. First, they worked on a new set of English words and agreed on the following:

Sounds the call to come together,

And united we shall stand.

Let us live and strive for freedom,

In South Africa, our land.

The revised version of our shortened national anthem was:

Nkosi Sikelel'iAfrika,

Maluphakanyisw'uphondo lwayo,

Yizwa imithandazo yethu,

Nkosi sikelela,

Thina lusapho lwayo.

Morena boloka setjhaba sa heso

Ofedise dintwa lematshwenyeho.

O se boloke, O se boloke,

Setjhaba sa heso,

Setjhaba sa South Africa.

SOUTH AFRICA

Uit die blou van onse hemel,

Uit die diepte van ons see,

Oor ons ewige gebergtes

Waar die kranse antwoord gee,

Sounds the call to come together,

And united we shall stand.

Let us live and strive for freedom

In South Africa, our land.

The anthem committee then gave the choral version of the completed anthem to Ms E.M. Hoeksma to add Tonic Sol-fa notes.

Then the committee considered other options of English and Afrikaans words. This they did not do with much relish because, almost to a man, they preferred the Afrikaans words of the first four lines of 'Die Stem' to those of its last four lines.

The committee did, however, work out another version as requested. In this second version, the first four lines of 'Die Stem' were in English, translated from Afrikaans and submitted by Mr H D Shaper of Cape Town. The complete text of this version was thus:

From our blue eternal heavens,

From the depths of our deepest sea.

From our everlasting mountains,

Comes the vow we make to thee!

Ons sal antwoord op jou roepstem,

Ons sal offer wat jy vra.

Ons sal lewe ons sal sterwe,

Ons vir jou Suid Afrika.

The committee decided to submit both versions to the Cabinet, but to recommend the adoption of the first.

Next, the committee revisited the versions of the choral groups. There were a number of beautiful settings of the shortened national anthem which all had one common flaw - they were musically too difficult to be sung by the general population and only suitable for choir performance. The committee prepared a special report on the version of two of the choirs the cabinet had made reference to, and arranged for recordings of their versions to be played at the next submission to the cabinet.

That submission was on the 17th May 1995. The cabinet accepted the first version. They also accepted the committee's assessment of other choral groups' versions.

The following day cabinet asked Dr Jeanne Zaidel-Rudolph to produce copies of the music and words.

On 10th June 1995, a parliamentary group known as Theme Committee One held a public hearing on "Seats of Government, Languages, and Names and Symbols" at the Old Assembly Chamber of Parliament in Cape Town. Professor Mzilikazi Khumalo, as the chairman of the anthem committee, was invited to make a submission on the national anthem. This was followed by a lively discussion in which members of Theme Committee One and most members of the public present expressed general satisfaction with the anthem committee's shortened national anthem.

The Springboks again!

The Springboks - the South African national rugby team - were again involved in some way in the singing of the two anthems as stated in the foregoing paragraph. It was on the 24th June 1995 during the final of the Rugby World Cup at Ellis Park involving the Springboks and New Zealand. The Springboks - captained by Francois Pienaar - made it a point of learning the words of "Nkosi Sikelel'iAfrika" and "Morena Boloka" - something they do with aplomb to date. As a result, when Imilonji ka Ntu (a choir from Soweto) led by Sibongile Khumalo and conducted by George Gobingca Mxadana, sang the two South African anthems just before the game started, the Springboks sang along from the beginning to the end. That rendition was in key G major from the beginning to the end, and the repetitions in "Nkosi Sikelel'iAfrika" and "Morena boloka" were eliminated, and the "Woza Moya" and "Makube njalo" sections were also eliminated. "Die Stem van Suid Afrika" was sung in its entirety.

CONCLUSION

In January 1997 Bonisudumo Choristers accompanied by the then National Symphony Orchestra and conducted by Richard Cock, performed the new version of the national anthem at the SABC M1A studio to an invited audience.

The following proclamation made the shortened version of "Nkosi Sikelel'iAfrika" and "Die Stem van Suid Afrika", as recommended by the anthem committee and accepted by cabinet, official:

In terms of Section 4 of the Constitution of South Africa, 1996 (Act 108 of 1996), and following Proclamation No. 68 in the Government Gazette No. 18341 (dated 10 October 1997), as printed in a Schedule to the Proclamation, a shortened, combined version of Nkosi Sikelel'iAfrika and The Call of South Africa in both Staff Notation and Tonic Solfa, is now the national anthem of South Africa.

Sir Seretse Khama, the first president of Botswana, stated that 'A nation without a past is a lost nation. And a people without a past is a people without a soul'. South Africa's national anthem, which embraces all the facets of its past, has also firmly set the course for a positive future.

BIBLIOGRAPHY

1. Jabavu, D.D.T. 1934, Introduction: Sontonga, E. Nkosi Sikelel'iAfrika Lovedale Sol-fa Leaflets No 17, Lovedale Press.

2. Imvo Zabansundu, June 27, 1905. Reeference found during a search for the death notice by G.M. Walker.

3. Smith, David James: Young Mandela. Kent: Weidenfeld & Nicolson, 2010.

4. Senekal, B.A. "Biografische gegevens". NEDWEB. Retrieved 2008-04-19.

5. Opland, Jeff. 'The First Novel in Xhosa'. Research in African Literatures, Volume 38, Number 4, Winter 2007, pp. 87-110.

6. Opland, Jeff (December 22, 2007). "The first novel in Xhosa. (S.E.K. Mqhayi USamson)". Indiana University Press. Retrieved 2006-08-10.

7. Barber, Karin (2006). Africa's Hidden Stories: Everyday Literacy and Making the Self. Indiana University Press. ISBN 0-253-34729-7.

8. Gerhart G.M. And Karis T. (ed) (1977). From Protest to challenge: A Documentary History of African Politics in South Africa: 1882-1964. Hoover Institution Pres: Stanford University.

9. Brownell, FG: National Symbols of the Republic of South Africa, 1995, Johannesburg: Chris van Rensburg Publications.

10. Department of Foreign Affairs and Information, 1983, South Africa 1983: Yearbook of the Republic of South Africa, 9th ed; Johannesburg: Chris van Rensburg Publications.

11. Republic of South Africa, 1994, Government Gazette, no 15694 of 1994, Pretoria: Government Printer.

12. Republic of South Africa, 1995, Government Gazette, no 1658 of 1995, Pretoria: Government Printer.

13. Republic of South Africa, 1997, Government Gazette, no 18341 of 1997, Pretoria: Government Printer.

14. South African Communication Service, 1993, South Africa 1993: Official Yearbook of the Republic of South Africa, 19th edition, Pretoria: South African Communication Service.

15. SAMRO Endowment for the Arts article on the national anthem.

16. Mothobi Mutloatse: Article: Healing a nation with a song.

17. South African History Online (SAHO).

18. National Monuments Council (Online).

19. Wikipedia.

20. Biographies - Hall of Fame (Online).

21. International Opus: Musical Diversity For New Millenium (Online).

22. Kwanzaa web.

23. Geneveve Walker: National Monuments Council; 1996.

24. SAMRO Archive of South African Music.

25. Article by Michael S. Levy - Consultant Musicologist: The South African National Anthem.

26. Article on South African Government Information.

27. Article from The Star: 18th April 2005.

28. Article from The Star: 6th May 1998.

29. Article from Beeld: 20th October 1976.

30. SAMRO report on Aspects of Copyright in The National Anthem.

31. Article by Michael S. Levy - Organiser: Serious Music - SAMRO: Nkosi Sikelel'iAfrika (1897) (and Die Stem); Information and material collected by Serious Music Department since 1976 as at 14th October 1994.

32. Copy of programme: NKOSI! The Healing Song.

33. Article by Professor Mzilikazi Khumalo: The National Anthem of South Africa.

34. Article from the Newsletter of the South African Choral Society; February 1996.

35. Article from the Sunday Times, 31ˢᵗ October 1993.

36. Article from Arts 1999, published by the Department of Arts, Culture, Science and Technology.

37. SAMRO Scores: South Africa Sings, Volume 1, 1998.

38. Article from Randburg Sun: 30ᵗʰ August 1996.

39. Article from The Star: 7ᵗʰ May 1996.

40. Article from The African Trust: NKOSI SIKELEL'IAFRIKA (The African Anthem).

41. Article from Departement van die Eerste Minister, Kaapstad; Mei 1957.

42. Article from The Star: 20ᵗʰ September 1994.

43. Article from The Star Tonight: 25th October 1994.

44. Article from the SAMRO Endowment for the National Arts: The story of the South African Anthem.

45. Article from Professor Jeanne Zaidel-Rudolph.

46. Professor Cherif Keita: Documentary film "From Inanda to Oberin: The Life and Times of John L. Dube.

Lightning Source UK Ltd.
Milton Keynes UK
UKOW02f0108100316

269912UK00002B/44/P